PRAY for YOUR CHURCH

30 Days Devoted to the Body of Christ

Stephen Brazzel

Copyright © 2017 Stephen Brazzel

All rights reserved. No part of this book may be used or reproduced by any means, graphic, electronic, or mechanical, including photoboypin, recordingg, taping or by any information storage retrieval system without the written permission of the author except in the case of brief quotations embeodied in critical articles and reviews.

Scripture taken from the Holman Christian Standard Bible* Copyright © 2003, 2002, 2000, 1999 by Holman Bible Publishers. All rights reserved.

Exposed To Christ Ministry books may be ordered through booksellers or by contacting:

ETC Ministries
219 Wickwood
Spring, TX 77386
www.exposedtochrist.com
713.907.0891

The views expressed in this work are solely those of the author and do not necessarily reflect the views of the publisher, and the publisher hereby disclaims any responsibility for them.

Any people depicted in stock images are being used for illustrative purposes only.

ISBN 978-0-9986648-0-4 (sc)

ETC Ministries rev. date 2/1/2017

FORMING A HEART FOR THE CHURCH

The purpose of this book is to help you become a prayer warrior on behalf of your church. Over the next thirty days we will spend time in God's Word seeing how both Jesus and Paul prayed for the church. We will use those prayers to teach you how you can pray for your church each day beyond the next month.

Jesus and Paul prayed for the church because the church is a holy endeavor. There are strategies, methods and wise practices that can be of assistance, but ultimately church is a spiritual undertaking. The power of the church isn't found in these methods and strategies. The power of the church is the hand of God moving among us. Therefore, it requires much prayer.

The church is in the middle of a great spiritual battle as the forces of Satan attempt to thwart the plan of God for humanity. Powers and principalities in high places are actively working against the church, at times within the church, to distract the church from its mission. The selfishness of humanity rises up to tear apart the fabric of unity in the church. Bitterness and frustration grow within the membership because the members of the church are frail and unable on their own to carry out the work of the church. Therefore, the church requires much prayer.

To be prepared for this we need much prayer. We don't need prayer to convince God to save people, because we know He already wants to do this. We don't need prayer to manipulate God into doing things on our behalf because we know He already wants to work in our lives.

We need prayer chiefly to prepare our own hearts to be ready for Him to work through us. We need prayer to align ourselves with His will. We need prayer to humble our hearts so that we will give Him proper glory and credit for what He does here. We need prayer to get ourselves out of His way. We need prayer to acknowledge our desperate need for Him to move in our midst. The journey begins and ends with God. Therefore, we need to pray.

My prayer for you as you work through the next thirty days is that God will use this book to challenge you and encourage you. I hope He begins to raise up prayer warriors for churches across the world who consistently enter His throne room on behalf of their local body of believers.

May God bless you richly as you pray for your church,
Stephen Brazzel

DAY 1
LORD, BE GLORIFIED IN YOUR CHURCH

John 17:1-5

Jesus spoke these things, looked up to heaven and said:

Father, the hour has come.
Glorify Your Son so that the Son may glorify You,
2 for You gave Him authority over all flesh;
so He may give eternal life to all You have given Him.
3 This is eternal life: that they may know You, the only true God, and the One You have sent—Jesus Christ.
4 I have glorified You on the earth by completing the work You gave Me to do.
5 Now, Father, glorify Me in Your presence with that glory I had with You before the world existed.

The night before His crucifixion Jesus prays for Himself, his disciples and the church that will be established after the coming of the Holy Spirit. John 17 is the record of this prayer, revealing this most personal moment between Him and His Father. This is where we begin, praying for the church as Jesus prayed for the church.

The first section of His prayer is dominated by the word "glorify." To glorify God is to make Him known or to cause others to acknowledge the dignity and worth of God. Jesus says, "Glorify Your Son so that the Son may glorify You." This prayer is unique to Jesus. We can't pray this because we are not worthy of glory, but Jesus is God in the flesh and He is worthy to be glorified. When the Father brings glory to Jesus He is also bringing glory to Himself.

The prayer of the believer is for the church to bring glory to both Jesus and the Father. We want to cause Him to become well known. We want the world, our neighbors, friends and enemies to acknowledge the Lord. This is how He is glorified.

This isn't about mere worship, though that is part of it. It is about making Him known in such a way that people are drawn to Him, not to us.

Jesus came, incarnate, surrendering His place and sacrificing His life to reveal the Father so that the world would be drawn to the Father. His intent was not judgment but revelation leading to salvation resulting in glorification. On this last night it meant complete surrender and sacrifice of self. It still means that. For God to be glorified we must surrender and sacrifice all.

When you pray for God to be glorified in your church, you must concurrently surrender yourself. You are giving God total control of your life and your church, your possessions and your preferences. You are inviting Him to become incarnate in you as Jesus was incarnate, God in flesh. You want Him to be seen and are willing to go anywhere, do anything for Him to be made known. You do this so that others will see Him and follow Him.

This isn't a rote prayer. This isn't a ritual prayer. This isn't a thoughtless prayer.

This is surrender.

Pray:
Lord, do whatever You need to do in me and in my church to bring Yourself glory. I surrender everything to

You. Your glory is more important than my comfort, my schedule, my possessions, or my life. To You be glory in the church.

_____

_____

_____

_____

_____

DAY 2
LORD, BE GLORIFIED IN YOUR CHURCH

John 17:1-5

Jesus spoke these things, looked up to heaven and said:
Father, the hour has come.
Glorify Your Son so that the Son may glorify You,
2 for You gave Him authority over all flesh;
so He may give eternal life to all You have given Him.
3 This is eternal life: that they may know You, the only true God, and the One You have sent—Jesus Christ.
4 I have glorified You on the earth \by completing the work You gave Me to do.
5 Now, Father, glorify Me in Your presence with that glory I had with You before the world existed.

Jesus said that He glorified His Father by "completing the work You gave Me to do." God is glorified through the church when the church completes the work He gives it. Listen to that again: God is glorified through the church when the church completes the work He gives it.

The only way the church can bring Him glory is by being obedient to the call of God. There are many good things a church can do that will benefit the community as well as its members, but if these are not God's call to the church then they do not bring Him glory. So how can you know what will bring Him glory in your church?

Do the basic things God has called the church to do. There are five things that are generally considered the functions of every church: Worship, Fellowship, Discipleship, Evangelism and Ministry. Pray for your church to be effective in these five things described in Acts 2:38-47. Pray for the church to be active in all five of these areas. Pray for the church to bring glory to God in each of these activities. Pray that these things are not done merely out of habit, but with a sincere desire to elevate the Lord, to cause others to know Him and follow Him.

Within these five functions there is a specific vision with specific strategies that God has for your church. This God given vision that God has for your church describes how your church will accomplish these basics unique to the body of Christ assembling together. While many churches may sing the same songs or participate in some of the same ministries, how your church does it will be unique to you and your calling.

The nature of God's vision for your church is that it will be challenging, requiring complete dependence upon Him and that it will bring Him glory.

Pray for your pastor, staff and leadership as they are continually seeking God's vision for your church. Pray that God will show them His desires for your body. Pray that God will reveal His plans that go beyond the bounds of what can be seen to the place of faith in an all-powerful Lord. Pray that He will grant them strength and boldness to lead the church to follow God's vision for the church.

Pray for members to embrace God's vision. Pray for the church to be obedient to God's call. There will be many temptations to settle for less or to shrink from the challenge of God's vision for your church. Pray that as

God challenges the church with the size of the vision that the church will continually put Him at the center. Remember, God's vision will always bring Him glory. When you follow the Lord, He will lead you outside your own abilities to make it clear to all that He deserves the glory.

Pray:
Lord, continue to show us Your vision, Your plan for our church. Burden us with obedience to Your plan. Keep us depending upon You to complete the work You have given us to do. Continue to reveal Your vision to our pastor and leadership. Give them courage and wisdom to lead our church to follow You.

_____

_____

_____

_____

_____

DAY 3
LORD, PROTECT YOUR CHURCH

John 17:9, 11-12, 15

9 I pray for them. I am not praying for the world but for those You have given Me, because they are Yours.
11 I am no longer in the world, but they are in the world, and I am coming to You. Holy Father, protect them by Your name that You have given Me, so that they may be one as We are one.
12 While I was with them, I was protecting them by Your name that You have given Me. I guarded them and not one of them is lost, except the son of destruction, so that the Scripture may be fulfilled.
15 I am not praying that You take them out of the world but that You protect them from the evil one.

Jesus is leaving. He has done all He can do with the disciples, leaving them a sure foundation with a certain faith. It is not hard to sense His desperation for the disciples. In verse 9 he says, "I pray for them." He knows what will come, how difficult it will be and how great the challenges will be.

Do not be surprised that the world hates the church. The world hated Christ and He predicted that they would hate His followers (John 15:18-25). The evil one (Satan) will attack the church (1 Peter 5:18). This doesn't mean that every difficulty or every conflict can be laid at the feet of the devil. More often than not we cause our own crises through our own selfish behavior. Where Satan chooses to focus is how we respond to challenges. He takes a small thing and makes it bigger, keeping our eyes focused on ourselves instead of the Savior. We look inward to take care of us instead of looking outward to take care of others. All of this will happen.

Jesus prays, not that everything goes smoothly or that problems cease to exist, but that the Lord will protect the church. He prays in verse 11, "protect them by Your name that You have given Me." In verse 12 he says, "I was protecting them by Your name that You have given Me. I guarded them." Again in verse 15 he prays, "I am not praying that You take them out of the world but that You protect them from the evil one."

The need for the Lord's protection should remind you that you are involved in a spiritual battle. Your church is in the middle of a spiritual battle at all times. Satan is not sitting by just waiting for the end, he is working every day to destroy you and your church. He wants to tear down the leadership of your church. He wants to dismantle the unity of your church. He wants to cause doubt among the young believers, resentment among the seasoned believers and frustration among all the believers. Satan wants you to become selfish, self-centered and self-obsessed. He wants to destroy the families within your church, to break up marriages and to alienate children from their parents.

So pray that the Lord will protect the church from these attacks. Pray that He will preserve the unity (more on that later). Pray that He will protect the pastor, staff and leadership of the church. Pray that He will keep you from destructive sin. Pray that He will guard you against the attacks of Satan. Just as Jesus prayed for the disciples, pray now for your church, not to escape the world but to be protected from the evil one.

Pray:
Lord, please protect my church from the attacks of the evil one. Keep us pure and unified. Guard our hearts from destructive attitudes and selfishness. Watch over our families and keep them centered on You. Protect us in the midst of spiritual battles. Lord, help us look to You for strength as we go through conflict and crisis.

_____

_____

_____

_____

_____

DAY 4
LORD, SANCTIFY YOUR CHURCH
John 17:14-19

¹⁴ I have given them Your word. The world hated them because they are not of the world, as I am not of the world.
¹⁵ I am not praying that You take them out of the world but that You protect them from the evil one.
¹⁶ They are not of the world, as I am not of the world.
¹⁷ Sanctify them by the truth; Your word is truth.
¹⁸ As You sent Me into the world, I also have sent them into the world.
¹⁹ I sanctify Myself for them, so they also may be sanctified by the truth.

Jesus is clear in His prayer about the relationship between His followers and the world. Like Him, those who follow Him are "not of the world." That is, their being is now distinct from the world. They are different from the world by composition. They are "new creations" as Paul would later say in 2 Corinthians 5:17. They have been changed.

Also like Him, those who follow Him have been sent "into the world." Though their composition may be different, their existence is not separate from the world. The challenge then, for those who are not of the world but sent into the world, is to be protected from the evil one and sanctified so that they do not become like the world.

To be sanctified is to be made holy and pure, to be set apart for the work of God. Twice Jesus prays that the church would be sanctified "by the truth." The prayer is not that the church would be quarantined and sanitized from the infections plaguing society, but that it would be sanctified by God's truth in the midst of society.

This is the work of God. We cannot sanctify ourselves, God must sanctify us. The church must be washed with the water of the Word (Ephesians 5:26) so that it can do the work God has planned for it. The Father will use His word, as it is preached and taught, to cleanse His church and to mold His church for His purposes. This means of course that there is sin from which we need to be cleansed. There must be repentance for a church to be sanctified. There must be a spirit of humility and a desperate longing for the holiness of God to be manifest in the body. There must be a willingness to be confronted by the truth and a desire to be set apart for His use. There must be brokenness and space for healing. Pride cannot be allowed to stifle the work of the redeeming Spirit.

When you begin to pray for the Lord to sanctify your church you are seeking to see these things happen within your church. Before they can happen in your church they must happen in your life. You must be humble before the Lord, asking Him to reveal any sin in your own life. You need to long for Him. You need to open His word and allow Him to confront your own failures and set you apart for His work.

Take some time today to sit before the Lord in humility and give Him space to break you and to heal you. Tell Him that you will set aside your pride to listen to what He has to say to you about your own walk. Once you have prayed for yourself, then talk to Him about your church.

Pray:
Lord, sanctify Your church by Your word. Anoint our pastor to preach Your word with power and truth. Break our hearts from any sin that is keeping us from following You. Give us a spirit of humility and desperation as we seek to be obedient to You. Lord, make us like You. Make us a people set apart for You, to be used by You, for Your glory.

_____

_____

_____

_____

_____

DAY 5
LORD, MAKE US UNITED AS A CHURCH

John 17:20-26

20 I pray not only for these, but also for those who believe in Me through their message.
21 May they all be one, as You, Father, are in Me and I am in You. May they also be one in Us, so the world may believe You sent Me.
22 I have given them the glory You have given Me. May they be one as We are one.
23 I am in them and You are in Me. May they be made completely one, so the world may know You have sent Me and have loved them as You have loved Me.
24 Father, I desire those You have given Me to be with Me where I am. Then they will see My glory, which You have given Me because You loved Me before the world's foundation.
25 Righteous Father! The world has not known You. However, I have known You, and these have known that You sent Me.
26 I made Your name known to them and will make it known, so the love You have loved Me with may be in them and I may be in them.

There may be no greater plague in churches over the centuries than the lack of unity. Disunity, factions, cliques and competing agendas have caused much heartache in churches and created poor reputations for churches in many communities. Unbelievers look at the arguments within a church and have no desire to be part of a group that claims righteousness but exhibits little love for one another. Jesus was fully aware of this challenge for the church for even His own disciples suffered disagreements and disharmony at times. The early church was no different than the 21st century church with its numerous schisms.

Therefore, we must be diligent to pray for the unity of the church and we will do so over the next three days. We will pray for unity along three different lines: relational, spiritual and missional.

Unity does not mean that everyone is exactly the same. Uniformity is not the unity sought by the Spirit. Unity is also not merely being joined together like two cats with their tails tied together. The cats may be unified in body but they will not be a model of cooperation. True unity is when those who are different, with different backgrounds, skills, cultures, likes, personalities and roles commit to follow the leadership of the Lord together and allow Him to mold their differences into a focused body of believers committed to the task He has assigned them.

The model for church unity is no less than the Trinity – Father, Son, Holy Spirit. Three persons in One God. The ability to understand the Trinity is limited by the inability to describe it accurately. Jesus gives us some insight in verses 21-23 of John 17. He prays, "You, Father, are in Me and I am in You... May they be one as We are one... I am in them and you are in Me. May they be made completely one."

Though the Father and the Son are vastly different, they are relationally one. They are in harmony with one another. They have different roles yet are together. This is the goal of the church, to be together in harmony even though we are each different with different roles, personalities and gifts.

Paul describes the church in 1 Corinthians 12 as a body with many parts but all part of one body. The church is designed to work together and the various parts are integral to the design. The entire body cannot be an eye or an arm. All the parts are needed and important and all should be appreciated and included.

When you look at the members of your church remember that each one is needed and placed there by God. Each one should be included and encouraged to actively use their gifts for the glory of the Lord. Show appreciation for each one and do things to build the unity of the body. Pray for each one and trust the Lord to build His body as He pleases.

Pray for the unity of the body, the unity of relationships. Pray for harmony in the body, that everyone will appreciate the various members of the body and include them all in the life of the body. Pray for relationships to be healed that are broken. Pray for forgiveness, humility and joy to pervade the fellowship.

Pray:
Lord, make us one as You and the Father are one. Fill us with Your Spirit and help us to see one another through Your eyes. Give us a spirit of humility as we work alongside one another. Heal the broken relationships that harm our fellowship. Help us work through conflict instead of avoiding it. Help us solve conflict under Your leadership instead of running away from it. Lord, deliver us from pride that keeps us from forgiveness.

DAY 6
LORD, MAKE US UNITED AS A CHURCH

John 17:20-26

20 I pray not only for these, but also for those who believe in Me through their message.
21 May they all be one, as You, Father, are in Me and I am in You. May they also be one in Us, so the world may believe You sent Me.
22 I have given them the glory You have given Me. May they be one as We are one.
23 I am in them and You are in Me. May they be made completely one, so the world may know You have sent Me and have loved them as You have loved Me.
24 Father, I desire those You have given Me to be with Me where I am. Then they will see My glory, which You have given Me because You loved Me before the world's foundation.
25 Righteous Father! The world has not known You. However, I have known You, and these have known that You sent Me.
26 I made Your name known to them and will make it known, so the love You have loved Me with may be in them and I may be in them.

We recognize that for a short period of time people have unified around various causes. Football teams, political campaigns, work groups and military units have all experienced unity in various degrees, for various causes and for various lengths of time. The need for relational unity in the church is one of the greatest needs in the local church today. But Jesus does not pray for unity based on just anything. He prays that the church would be unified with one another as they are also in unity with Him and the Father.

In verse 21 He says, "May they also be one in Us." In verse 23, "I am in them and You are in Me." In verse 24, "I desire those You have given Me to be with Me where I am." In verse 26, "I may be in them."

Jesus prays that His followers would remain intimately connected to Him in spiritual unity. He wants the church to be completely unified to Him and so they will be unified with one another. He will not be satisfied with unity among believers based on anything other than relationship with Him.

Your spiritual walk with Christ impacts the potential for unity within the body. As members walk more faithfully with the Lord they grow closer to Him and become more committed to His work in the church. This growing commitment enhances the unity of the church. Each member is responsible for their own relationship and unity with Christ, and so each can enhance the unity of the church.

Growth is not an individual sport though. We grow together as we worship together, work together, study together in small groups, do ministry together, observe the ordinances together, pray together and strive together to overcome adversity. Your personal growth will be limited by your willingness to be in community with others through a local church. There are some things about God you can only learn while in community with others. There are some things that God wants to teach you through others in the local church. Your personal growth is tied to your commitment to the local community of believers.

Praying for the unity of the church means you are committing to be involved in the church and to go through the travails of life together with the community of the local church. Praying for unity means you are committed to personal spiritual growth and you are seeking to see the local body grow closer to the Lord together. Praying for unity means you are committed to the Lord's work through your local church and you are willing to work through the struggles of relationship as members grow in the various stages of spiritual maturity. Praying for unity means you recognize that everyone is important even though they may not look or act like you and may not like the same things or even worship to the same music. Praying for unity means you are committed to the Lord through the local church.

Pray:
Lord, grow our church spiritually. Deepen our walk with you as individuals and as a body. Challenge us to seek unity and to embrace one another despite our differences. Teach us to love one another. Lord teach me about Your love for me as I learn to love my church family. Lord teach me about your forgiveness of me as I forgive and am forgiven by others.

_____

_____

_____

_____

_____

DAY 7
LORD, MAKE US UNITED AS A CHURCH

John 17:20-26

20 I pray not only for these, but also for those who believe in Me through their message.
21 May they all be one, as You, Father, are in Me and I am in You. May they also be one in Us, so the world may believe You sent Me.
22 I have given them the glory You have given Me. May they be one as We are one.
23 I am in them and You are in Me. May they be made completely one, so the world may know You have sent Me and have loved them as You have loved Me.
24 Father, I desire those You have given Me to be with Me where I am. Then they will see My glory, which You have given Me because You loved Me before the world's foundation.
25 Righteous Father! The world has not known You. However, I have known You, and these have known that You sent Me.
26 I made Your name known to them and will make it known, so the love You have loved Me with may be in them and I may be in them.

Unity among the members of the church is based on a growing relationship with the Lord Jesus Christ. Unity among the members is not for the sake of unity. Jesus prays knowing that unity will become a key part of the testimony about who He is. In verses 21 and 23 he prays for His followers to be one "so that the world may believe (know) You sent Me." We have prayed for unity in relationship with one another and with Christ. Today we pray for unity that furthers the mission.

Ultimately everything the church does is about the mission of bringing others to faith in Christ. Jesus' mission has become our mission. He came for the world. He came so that the world would know the Father. The mission is always primary. When we prayed for the church to glorify Christ, this was the accomplishment of the mission – that others would acknowledge and follow Christ.

Unity is a key to the accomplishment of the mission of Christ. He prays for unity of the church knowing that the world will be drawn to any assembly that will work together in spite of obvious differences between the members. The world says it wants to live in harmony, to find a place of peace. That place of peace should be the church, can only be the church. Only in the church can real harmony and peace be found because these are only found in Christ.

Pray for unity in the church so that the church can be a bright beacon shining to a world in chaotic conflict. Everywhere you look people are arguing, hating, demanding uniformity and punishing dissent. The church in unity can offer a redeeming gospel that receives people from all walks of life, gives them peace and transforms them into a loving, forgiving body of believers. This is what the world says it wants and it can only be found in the church.

Pray for unity in the church around the mission. Pray that everyone in the church would place the mission of the church above all else. Pray for unity in the church to accomplish the work of the church in the world. Pray that the name of Christ would become great in the world through the life of the church.

Pray:
Lord, unify our church so that we might make Your name well known in our community. Draw us together as we reach out to the lost world. Help us put aside our differences so that we might impact the lives of those who don't know You. Lord, we want Your agenda to be first and only before us. Forgive us for putting our desires before Yours. Unify us Lord. Make us Your church for this world.

_____

_____

_____

_____

_____

DAY 8
LORD, FILL US WITH KNOWLEDGE OF YOU

Colossians 1:9-12

9 For this reason also, since the day we heard this, we haven't stopped praying for you. We are asking that you may be filled with the knowledge of His will in all wisdom and spiritual understanding, 10 so that you may walk worthy of the Lord, fully pleasing to Him, bearing fruit in every good work and growing in the knowledge of God. 11 May you be strengthened with all power, according to His glorious might, for all endurance and patience, with joy 12 giving thanks to the Father, who has enabled you to share in the saints' inheritance in the light.

Read through the book of Acts and you will see clearly that Paul was the greatest evangelist and church planter in the history of the church. Read through the letters of Paul found in the New Testament and it will become clear that Paul was not only a great theologian but also a man of prayer. Paul's prayer list was long and his prayers for the church showed his love for and knowledge of the needs of the church.

In this passage from Colossians 1, Paul gives three descriptions related to his prayer for the Colossians: knowledge of His will, wisdom and spiritual understanding. We need to grow continually in our knowledge of His will through studying His word. The best way to know what God wants is to read and understand His word. Pray for your pastor and all of the teachers in your church. Pray for those who work with children and youth to teach them the truth from God's Word. Pray that the church will be filled with the knowledge of Christ.

We also need wisdom which could be described as the faithful application of the truth and principles found in His word. You might say to pray for our knowledge that we know WHAT to do and wisdom that we know HOW to do it. Pray that God's Word would be properly applied to the church and to individual lives.

Many people in church know what they are supposed to do. They know right from wrong and can easily identify things the Lord would have them do from those things that would displease Him. The struggle we have is actually doing the right things. We rebel against our own knowledge and our acquired wisdom. Pray that the church would not only know what and how to do, but that it would be obedient to God's word. Knowledge is always tied to obedience in the word of God.

Spiritual understanding is the ability to discern the circumstances and actively apply God's wisdom to them. We need our churches to be filled with people who rightly apply God's word to current situations. Too often believers use human based wisdom and secular principles to solve life struggles. Pray that your church will seek God's wisdom and apply true spiritual discernment to every situation. Pray that your church will have knowledge, wisdom and spiritual understanding.

Pray:
Lord, fill us with the knowledge of You and Your will. Speak to our pastor and teachers as they study and prepare. Guide them into Your truth and give us a holy

hunger for Your Word. Help us apply Your Word. We need to be doers of the word and not hearers only. We need Your wisdom. We need to know You.

_____

_____

_____

_____

_____

DAY 9
LORD, GROW YOUR CHURCH

Colossians 1:9-12

9 For this reason also, since the day we heard this, we haven't stopped praying for you. We are asking that you may be filled with the knowledge of His will in all wisdom and spiritual understanding, 10 so that you may walk worthy of the Lord, fully pleasing to Him, bearing fruit in every good work and growing in the knowledge of God. 11 May you be strengthened with all power, according to His glorious might, for all endurance and patience, with joy 12 giving thanks to the Father, who has enabled you to share in the saints' inheritance in the light.

We need to be filled with wisdom, but God isn't interested in growing a cathedral of spiritual PhD candidates who don't apply the Word. Paul prays that we might "walk worthy of the Lord." Knowledge is never just for knowing. Pray for your church to consistently walk in faith in the community.

The standard is high. Paul's prayer is not for the church to be filled with good people, but people who walk "worthy of the Lord." Knowledge of Him and His wisdom leads you to transformation. Your life path is different, your goals are different, your values are different. Pray that your church is filled with people who are being transformed (Romans 12:1-2) by the power of God.

Paul goes on to call this living in a way that is "fully pleasing" to Him. It is a great challenge for us to walk in a way that pleases the Lord (Ephesians 5:10). Be gracious, forgiving, humble. Walk with integrity. Rejoice. Pray that your church is fully pleasing to the Lord in everything it does. Pray that the worship pleases the Lord. Pray that the church has a forgiving and generous spirit. Pray that the church upholds righteousness. Pray that the church does WHAT God wants, HOW He wants it done and WHERE He wants it done.

When God instills His truth and His people are obedient, the church will bear fruit. Certainly He means that we should bear the fruit of the Spirit (Gal 5:22-23) but also He means that we should grow. Pray for new converts, new believers. Pray that the church would multiply. Pray that God would make your church a place of transformation for those who are in darkness. Pray that God would use your church to minister to the broken, visit the lonely, love the outcast and raise up the downtrodden. Pray that those you share the gospel with would be ready to respond. Pray that God would prepare their hearts today to hear the gospel and to come to faith.

Pray:
Lord, make Your will clear to us and guide us as we seek to be obedient to You. We need to follow You. We want to please You. We want to see people come to saving faith in Your Son, Jesus Christ. Lord, show us the world around us and give us an unending burden for it. Please prepare the hearts of our neighbors as we reach out to them. Lord, grow Your church.

DAY 10
LORD, STRENGTHEN YOUR CHURCH

Colossians 1:9-12

9 For this reason also, since the day we heard this, we haven't stopped praying for you. We are asking that you may be filled with the knowledge of His will in all wisdom and spiritual understanding, 10 so that you may walk worthy of the Lord, fully pleasing to Him, bearing fruit in every good work and growing in the knowledge of God. 11 May you be strengthened with all power, according to His glorious might, for all endurance and patience, with joy 12 giving thanks to the Father, who has enabled you to share in the saints' inheritance in the light.

Paul prays for the church in Colosse to be strong in the power of God. The church must endure hardship with patience, joy and thanksgiving.

No one gets to spend a lot of time on the mountaintop. Most of our lives are spent going up and coming down. This is where we need strength and endurance. If life was easy we would not need to endure. We enjoy pleasure; we endure hardship. This applies to the church as well as the individual.

When we go through the difficult days God fills us with power. Therefore, we shouldn't want to avoid hardship, as if we could, because we know those are the moments God shows Himself through us. Don't pray for your church to always have days of calm, it won't be like that anyway. Pray for your church to experience God's power and strength when you are weak.

Trusting in His power in those days results in patience, joy and thanksgiving. By faith we know God will give us strength to endure. Therefore, we can be patient, waiting for him to do what He will do. He will not disappoint when you wait on Him (Psalm 27:14). Pray for your church to trust in His power, not their resources.

When your church sees God deliver on His promises then you will experience overwhelming joy and thanksgiving. Your church needs to experience the true joy of seen faith. Pray for the Lord to pour His strength through your church. Pray for your church to be dependent on the Lord.

Pray:
Lord, we need You. We need You to do Your work in us. We need Your wisdom, Your strength so that we might walk worthy of You. We want to please You. Bear Your fruit in our lives. Bear Your fruit through our lives. Lord help us to trust You, to follow You, to love what You love, to be strong in Your power. Lord, we need You.

_____

_____

_____

_____

DAY 11
LORD, BURDEN YOUR CHURCH

Colossians 1:13-14

13 He has rescued us from the domain of darkness and transferred us into the kingdom of the Son He loves. 14 We have redemption, the forgiveness of sins, in Him.

Paul's prayer for the church in Colosse finishes with a reminder of what the Lord has done for us. In verses 13 and 14 he talks about the work of Christ on our behalf that put us into the church. He says, "He rescued us ... and transferred us" and in Christ "we have redemption." All of these words describe an act of God on our behalf. These are all things that God has done and that only God can do.

He rescued us from the deep darkness of lostness. Without Him we were living in darkness and had no ability to see truth, reach out for love or embrace grace. We were lost. But then God rescued us and transferred us from darkness into His kingdom. Suddenly we found ourselves in the light, surrounded by grace and overwhelmed by His love. This is redemption and we are completely reliant upon God for it.

This is God's work done for each one of us. We have a common heritage that isn't affected by our social status, adjusted gross income, racial background, national allegiance or gender. He is continuing this work in the lives of millions today as He continues to call the lost to Himself. He is still seeking those in darkness and redeeming those in need of forgiveness.

As we saw a couple of days ago, because this is solely a work of God, we must pray. We pray for the church to remember who we were and what God has done for us. We pray the church will be humble before God, seeing that we all shared the same lostness.

Understanding that we all come from the same place should also help us see that those outside the faith now are in the same spiritual place we once were. Perhaps it would be good to see them not as the lost but as pre-believers. Our prayer is that once they hear the gospel they will turn to God in faith to be rescued from darkness. Pray for the church to consistently reach out to pre-believers, sharing the redemption found only in Christ. Pray that the church remain humble before pre-believers, knowing that our place is because of Christ, not ourselves. Pray that the church be welcoming to those outside the faith, opening the doors of faith to those who think they are too different for God to know or love them.

Pray for the gospel message to be proclaimed clearly by the church in both words and deeds. Pray that the light of the gospel would shine brightly through the lives of church members. Pray that the church would have a God-sized burden for those in the community who have not yet heard or believed the gospel.

Pray:
Lord, thank You for saving me, for rescuing me, for redeeming me and forgiving me. Thank you for not giving up on me and for putting people in my life who would share Your love with me. I pray our church would continually reach out to those who have yet to believe in You. Burden our hearts for the lost, the pre-believers.

Remind us of what You have done in us and what You want to do in the lives of many more. Please keep our eyes focused on Your desire for the world around us.

_____

_____

_____

_____

_____

DAY 12
LORD, THANK YOU FOR YOUR CHURCH

Ephesians 1:15-16

15 This is why, since I heard about your faith in the Lord Jesus and your love for all the saints, 16 I never stop giving thanks for you as I remember you in my prayers.

Gratitude should be a consistent part of our walk with God. As he begins this letter to the church in Ephesus Paul reminds us to give thanks for the people in our lives. He mentions how the Ephesians have been faithful to the Lord and have a great love for one another ("all the saints"). These are traits that identify them as believers and hold them together as a church body. Certainly we know people who have these traits and have exhibited them toward us.

Start a list of those who have made an impact on your walk with Christ. Think about the people in your life who have encouraged you when you were struggling. Put on your list believers who challenge you to grow deeper. Remember to list friends who have been used by God to teach you His truth.

Paul consistently gives thanks for the churches. He thanks the Lord for their faith and their love. These are churches who have problems, who struggle, who act without faith at times. Yet Paul finds ways to give thanks for them. He knows they are not perfect, yet he does not withhold his thanksgiving until they become perfect.

One of the challenges of growing up comes when we realize that our parents are not perfect, or our favorite teacher has faults, or the pastor does not wear angel wings under his shirt. We should not fail to recognize the positive impact people have had on our lives just because we are aware of their shortcomings. Give thanks for how God has redeemed them and used them. Give thanks for their walk with the Lord.

Take time today to thank Him for family, friends and others who have presented you with a godly witness. Thank Him for how they have influenced you and how they have blessed you. Thank God for how He has used these people to push and prod you to live for His glory. Thank Him for their faith and love for the church. Let's agree together no matter the hardships and trials that are going to come, we will always be thankful for one another.

Pray:
Lord, thank You for Your church. Thank You for the good things they have done and how they have pushed me toward You. Thank You for using them to draw others to faith. Thank You for their love and their faith. Thank You for the difference they have made in this community.

My list of people who have blessed me:

_____

_____

_____

_____
_____
_____
_____
_____
_____
_____
_____

DAY 13
LORD, REVEAL YOURSELF TO YOUR CHURCH

Ephesians 1:17

17 I pray that the God of our Lord Jesus Christ, the glorious Father would give you a spirit of wisdom and revelation in the knowledge of Him.

Paul continues his prayer by asking God to reveal Himself and His will to the believers. We need to know God in great depth and intimacy. If life were a great game of hide and seek and God was "it," we would never find Him. He must reveal Himself to us. So we pray, asking God to show Himself, to reveal His will to the church.

But we also need to have a desire, a spirit, that wants to know Him. One of the reasons we pray is to give evidence to ourselves of our own desire to know God. We need Him more than anything. Jesus prayed and fasted 40 days in the desert and then responded to Satan's temptation by quoting, "Man must not live on bread alone but on every word that comes from the mouth of God." (Matt 4:4)

God's word, His revelation of Himself, is the only source of eternal life there is. We must hunger for it like we hunger for the next meal. We must thirst after Him and

His wisdom as if we were walking across a great desert looking for water. Pray that your church would hunger and thirst after the Lord and His wisdom. Pray that people would commit themselves to Bible study, both at home and in corporate settings like small group Bible studies and worship times. Pray that hunger for knowledge of Him would be so great in your church that people would wake up early to get to worship on time.

We do not want to settle for cheap substitutes to the knowledge of God. We don't want to be satisfied with surface devotion. We will not be content with mere ritual. We are praying for greater desire to know God. We want a spiritual transformation to take place. Our focus is not to design a more exciting worship service but to desire a deeper understanding of God, to hunger for His presence.

We know that this is a prayer that the Lord is eager to answer in our lives. He wants to reveal Himself to us and He is waiting for us to seek Him earnestly. He will show Himself and pour His wisdom into the heart and mind of a church that sincerely desires to know Him.

Pray:
Ask the Lord to give you a desire for Him. Ask Him to create in your heart a hunger and thirst for righteousness. Examine your heart to see if there are cheap substitutes you have accepted in place of a knowledge of Him. Pray that God would replace your desires for the shallow with a "spirit of wisdom and revelation in the knowledge of Him." Pray that your church would seek Him and that He would reveal Himself to you.

_____

_____

DAY 14
LORD, OPEN THE EYES OF YOUR CHURCH

Ephesians 1:18-19

18 I pray that the perception of your mind may be enlightened so you may know what is the hope of His calling, what are the glorious riches of His inheritance among the saints, 19 and what is the immeasurable greatness of His power to us who believe, according to the working of His vast strength.

Paul prays for the church to have a new understanding about God's call, His resources and His power. One of the keys to your growth and preparation for God's work in your life is that you need to have a proper understanding, or perception, of who God is and what God will do.

Probably one of the greatest limiters in the life of a Christian is that we put God in a small box that matches our past experiences. This box can limit the scope of God's work because we think He will always work the same way He has in the past. It can limit the power of God because we only ask Him to do like He has done in our past. It can limit our submission to God because we are only seeking to be obedient to Him like we have in the past.

This is what Paul talked about in Romans 12 when he exhorted the church to be "transformed by the renewing of your mind" (Romans 12:2). The mind of the church and the church member must be transformed. We cannot allow our human thinking to impede on the work God desires to do among us and through us. We must seek His thoughts, His ways and His mind. Godly thinking is fundamental to our ability to be obedient. We will not follow the Lord with abandon until we begin to see ourselves and the world as He does.

Prepare yourself for His thoughts to become your thoughts. The Lord doesn't look at the world the same way we do. He sees others through the lens of perfect love as His unique creations. He knows conflict is the place for growth. He has a creative view at all times so His solutions are unique and His work is flawless. He knows us and He uses our limitations to reveal Himself to the world. When you ask Him to enlighten your mind you must be prepared for a new way of thinking and doing.

This new way is exactly what our churches need. You need to ask God to enlighten your mind and that of your church. This begins today and needs to continue throughout your life. You need God to broaden your idea of how He can use you. Ask Him to reveal the ways you have tried to limit Him in the past. Confess your lack of trust. Ask God to begin to expand your vision of what He can do through you. Ask Him to help you see others through His eyes. See them as He does, with perfect love.

The great challenge in prayer is for the corporate body of the church to be enlightened. Individual members, pastoral leaders and others may see what the Lord does, but the body needs to see as the Lord does for the church to move the culture toward the Lord. So pray for yourself, but pray also for the church. When the vision from the Lord overtakes the church, then the community and world around the church will be transformed forever.

Pray:
Lord, open our eyes to see as you see. Help us put aside our vision of ourselves to adopt Your vision. Forgive us for limiting You in the past. We want to see You. We want to see our future as You see it. We need Your eyes. Expand our vision.

_____

_____

_____

_____

_____

DAY 15
LORD, YOU ARE OUR HOPE

Ephesians 1:18-19

18 I pray that the perception of your mind may be enlightened so you may know what is the hope of His calling, what are the glorious riches of His inheritance among the saints, 19 and what is the immeasurable greatness of His power to us who believe, according to the working of His vast strength.

Hope.

Hope is a powerful word. It is a word of life. Without hope we shrink down into the pit of despair, trials overtake us and vitality leaks from us. Without hope we devolve into anger, bitterness, regret, licentiousness and lust. Without hope we quit on others and ourselves.

Those full of hope are always looking forward. The hopeful believe there is a day coming that will bring deliverance, rescue, redemption and joy. The hopeful are certain that they are not forgotten. They know God is powerful enough and infinitely loving. They trust that God will act on their behalf. They are sure of His promises.

For the believer, hope is not limited to the sweet by and by, but we believe in hope for today. Paul prayed that the church would know the "hope of His calling." He prayed that intellectual understanding would become heartfelt confidence in the power and will of God to rescue His children.

Paul knew the Lord as His deliverer. He knew the Lord as the One who would continue to work through the lives of believers to accomplish His purpose. He prays that the church will trust the Lord and put their hope in the Lord.

Remember, Paul wrote Philippians 1:6: "Being confident of this, that he who began a good work in you will carry it on to completion until the day of Christ Jesus." He wrote Ephesians 2:10: "For we are God's workmanship, created in Christ Jesus to do good works, which God prepared in advance for us to do." He wrote Galatians 6:9: "Let us not become weary in doing good, for at the proper time we will reap a harvest if we do not give up." He wrote Romans 8:37-39: "No, in all these things we are more than conquerors, through him who loved us. For I am convinced that neither death nor life, neither angels nor demons, neither the present nor the future, nor any powers, neither height nor depth, nor anything else in all creation, will be able to separate us from the love of God that is in Christ Jesus our Lord."

Paul knows his Lord and he is convinced that God will not abandon his children. Not that he still doesn't struggle with faith, but in his heart he is convinced that God will deliver. So he asks for prayers for strength and faith and gives thanks for those prayers in advance. We should not only act in faith on our own, but also pray for others that they too may display faith in God and trust in him for deliverance. God will not disappoint. Put your hope in God. Pray that the church will place their hope in God.

We may look at budget shortfalls and failing attendance and wonder if there is any hope for the church. Conflict among church members may darken our outlook and cultural shifts may lead us to think the day for the church has passed. Don't lose hope. Trust the Lord. He is able. He will not leave the church alone in the world.

Pray:
Lord, we place our hope in You. No matter the crisis or how great the challenge we know You love us and will act to accomplish Your will in us. We know You are our Deliverer. We trust in You. We want to know the Hope of Your calling.

_____

_____

_____

_____

_____

DAY 16
LORD, WE ARE YOUR INHERITANCE

Ephesians 1:18-19

18 I pray that the perception of your mind may be enlightened so you may know what is the hope of His calling, what are the glorious riches of His inheritance among the saints, 19 and what is the immeasurable greatness of His power to us who believe, according to the working of His vast strength.

In verse 18 Paul talks about the "glorious riches of His inheritance among the saints." Read it closely again. Chapter 1 of Ephesians, verse 14, talks about our inheritance. Christ is the down payment on our inheritance. In verse 18 Paul is talking about the glorious riches of His inheritance. So what is His inheritance? We are.

Those who have put their faith and trust in Jesus Christ as Lord and Savior become His inheritance. We are His treasured possession (Psalm 135:4; 1 Peter 2:9). We are a gift to Him from the Father (John 17:9, 11-12). Did you realize this? Did you know that you are a gift to Christ, that you are His inheritance, that you are considered part of His glorious riches?

The church is precious to God. We are more valuable to Him than a diamond ring is to a bride. We are so valuable that God sent His Son to purchase us by dying on the cross. No matter the size of the church, it is valuable to Him. No matter the resources of the church, it is precious to Him. No matter the socio-economic status of the church, He loves it and protects it. Pray that the church understands how important it is to the Father and the Son. We are His inheritance.

This is an amazing truth that should be embraced by all believers. God sees the church as a part of His infinite wealth which brings glory to His name. Therefore, God should gain glory from His wealth, the church.

The Message Bible translates this part of the verse like this: "grasp the immensity of this glorious way of life he has for Christians." Pray for the church to grab hold of their place as the inheritance of Christ and that this means we should bring glory to Him. With all of His resources at our disposal, we have the great privilege of leading the way in bringing praise to the Father and the Son. Pray that the church lives in a manner worthy of the Lord. Pray that we reflect His glory to the world. Pray that others see the wonder of God when they look at your church.

Pray:
Lord, sometimes we look at ourselves with critical eyes, seeing only our faults and shortcomings. Lord, thank You for saving us and for loving us. Thank You for the great inheritance You have given us. Remind us how precious we are to You. Help us embrace our place in Your plan. Now Lord, make us worthy of You. Show us how we can bring glory to You. Lord, our desire is that others would see You when they look at our church.

_____

_____

_____

DAY 17
LORD, YOU ARE OUR POWER

Ephesians 1:18-21

18 I pray that the perception of your mind may be enlightened so you may know what is the hope of His calling, what are the glorious riches of His inheritance among the saints, 19 and what is the immeasurable greatness of His power to us who believe, according to the working of His vast strength. 20 He demonstrated this power in the Messiah by raising Him from the dead and seating Him at His right hand in the heavens— 21 far above every ruler and authority, power and dominion and every title given, not only in this age but also in the one to come.

As we continue through this passage notice the emphasis placed on the work of God among believers. In verse 19 he references the "greatness of His power to us who believe." God's work, His power, is directed to the lives of those who are His followers.

Today He is not focusing His work on parting seas and burning bushes, though He could. He has purposed to use His power through the Holy Spirit in the lives of those who are His followers. That's you and me. He wants to pour Himself out in your life and mine. He wants the world to see the greatness of His power by the things He does in us who believe.

His power, which cannot even be measured and was exhibited in the raising of Jesus from the dead, is at work in your life. Therefore, you are without excuse when it comes to following His leadership. You are filled with His power. If God has called you to obedience then He will accomplish His work through your life by His power. He is not dependent upon your ability to accomplish His will. He brings the ability, the strength, the resolve, the power to make anything happen within His will.

What is true for you is also true for your church. He fills your church with His power to accomplish His will. Too often we allow our perception of our resources and our abilities to limit our view of what can happen in our church. Remember, His church is powered by His Holy Spirit to do whatever He wills.

This is why we need to pray for our minds to see what He wants, to know the hope of his calling. Pray that your church has a clear vision of His will which pushes the church beyond their own limitations to be completely reliant upon Jesus Christ. Pray for your church to trust the powerful hand of God to accomplish His will among you and through you. Living in the space beyond our strength, where only God can make up the difference, is a scary place of faith. Here the church and the community see the power of God demonstrated and are drawn to follow a God who can do miracles.

Consider the things that God has spoken to you about your involvement in the church. Have you questioned God about why He may be asking you? Have you questioned your ability to do what you have heard Him ask? Read over these verses again and understand that God is not asking you to follow with your strength and ability but with His. Is there anything He cannot do through you? Be encouraged, God is calling you precisely because only He can do this through you. Only

He is able and He is eager to accomplish His will with you. He called you to follow on this journey because you are the one He wanted to work through.

Pray:
Lord, I want to live in the place where only You can do the work. Grow our faith as a church to trust You and Your power. Stretch us to be people of faith. Demonstrate Your power in us and through us to the world around us. Do the things that only You can do. We want to see You. We give You all the glory for Your work in Your church.

_____

_____

_____

_____

_____

DAY 18
LORD, BLESS OUR PASTOR

Ephesians 3:14-17

¹⁴ For this reason I kneel before the Father ¹⁵ from whom every family in heaven and on earth is named. ¹⁶ I pray that He may grant you, according to the riches of His glory, to be strengthened with power in the inner man through His Spirit, ¹⁷ and that the Messiah may dwell in your hearts through faith.

Dr. Wilbur Chapman often told of his experience when, as a young man, he became pastor of a church in Philadelphia. After his first sermon, an old gentleman said to him, "You're pretty young to be pastor of this church. But you preach the Gospel and I'm going to help you all I can." Dr. Chapman thought, "Here's a crank." But the man continued: "I'm going to pray for you that you may have the Holy Spirit's power upon you. Two others have covenanted to join with me in prayer for you." Dr. Chapman said, "I didn't feel so bad when I learned he was going to pray for me. The 3 became 10, the 10 became 20 and 20 became 50, the 50 became 200 who met before every service to pray that the Holy Spirit might come upon me. I always went into my pulpit feeling that I would have the anointing in answer to the prayers of those who had faithfully prayed for me. It was a joy to preach! The result was that we received 1,100 into our church by conversion in three years, 600 of whom were men. It was the fruit of the Holy Spirit in answer to prayer!"

Your pastor needs people like this praying for him every day and especially before he steps up to preach. The job of a pastor is a difficult job, like many other jobs. It is physically and mentally challenging as are many professions. But the spiritual challenge involved in pastoring a church is unlike any other job. Satan relishes the opportunity to destroy a pastor. He goes after the pastor from multiple fronts. He attacks his family, his personal life, his congregation and his staff. He sometimes uses members of the church to attack the pastor or members of the staff. He knows the weaknesses in the man who fills the pulpit and he works to exploit them every day. Your pastor needs your prayers!

He needs your prayers because what he is doing can only be accomplished through the power of the Holy Spirit. He needs the Spirit working in his inner man to anoint him to do this work. He must be a vessel for the Spirit to speak. He must be humble before the Lord to allow the Spirit to control his attitude and his actions as well as his words. He must be directed by the Spirit to lead the church under the Lordship of Christ. He must be sensitive to the needs of the congregation while also leading, prodding and sometimes pushing them to follow the Lord. He must be willing to ask others to sacrifice for the Lord. Your pastor needs your prayers!

Will you be one of those who will pray for your pastor? Will you commit to pray for him on a daily basis? Will you pray for him before and during each service? Will you pray for God's anointing on him? Will you encourage him by praying for him and sharing your prayers with him? The goal is not to exalt the pastor, but that the Holy Spirit will pour His power through him to bring people to salvation, to heal families and redeem that which seemed lost forever.

Pray:
Lord, anoint our pastor. Bless him with Your presence and Your leadership. Protect him and his family from attacks and help them to be strong spiritually under the stress of ministry. Bless him as he preaches Your word. Use him to accomplish Your will among us and give our church a generous spirit toward him. Help us be a blessing to him and to his family.

List the names of your pastor and his family along with each staff member and their families. Pray through this list on a regular basis.

_____

_____

_____

_____

_____

_____

_____

_____

_____

_____

DAY 19
LORD, DWELL IN YOUR CHURCH

Ephesians 3:14-17

14 For this reason I kneel before the Father 15 from whom every family in heaven and on earth is named. 16 I pray that He may grant you, according to the riches of His glory, to be strengthened with power in the inner man through His Spirit, 17 and that the Messiah may dwell in your hearts through faith.

As Paul prayed for the church and believers in Ephesus he prayed that the "Messiah may dwell in your hearts through faith." Since they were already believers he wasn't praying for their salvation. Since you can't lose your salvation, he wasn't praying that they remain believers. He was praying that they would continually make Christ "at home" in their lives. The word used there means to allow the Messiah to "pervade" and to "govern over." This is more than mere inhabitance. It is overwhelming presence and leadership.

When we think about the Lord "dwelling" in a church, we should be careful not to get stuck in the Old Testament. That is, in the Old Testament the Lord dwelled in the Temple. His presence was there in the Holy of Holies. He even left the Temple in Ezekiel 10. But we live under the New Covenant where the Spirit doesn't dwell in the building but in the people. Though we know there is something special about the place where God's people gather to worship together, whether that is a permanent facility, a school, hotel ballroom or a living room, the Lord now dwells in the hearts of his followers and among them wherever they gather.

The prayer we offer then is for the Lord to pervade the individual lives of believers and also to govern over their gatherings together. Pray for the Lord to have dominion over every area of life in the church and the church member. Pray that there would be no hidden places in our lives. Pray that we would not exclude His presence from any area of our existence. Pray that the church would seek to honor God in every activity and that every gathering would be filled with the presence of the Holy Spirit.

Are there areas of your life you are keeping from the Lord? Are there sins you are trying to hide or conceal from His all-knowing Spirit? Confess to Him and be forgiven. He loves you and wants the best for you. His best is perfect. Today give Him permission to govern over all areas of your life. Ask Him to be pervasive in your life, even the uncomfortable places and the previously hidden places. Ask Him to be Lord over your whole heart. Trust His grace.

Pray:
Lord, here is all of my life. I give You everything in me. Show me areas that I have kept away from You. Reveal anything I think I have hidden from You. Lord we need Your presence in our church. There is no good thing without You. We want You to fill our hearts with Your love, Your will, Your Spirit. We seek Your leadership in our lives together. Lord, dwell among us.

_____

_____

_____

DAY 20
LORD, THANK YOU FOR LOVING YOUR CHURCH

Ephesians 3:17-19

17 and that the Messiah may dwell in your hearts through faith. I pray that you, being rooted and firmly established in love, 18 may be able to comprehend with all the saints what is the length and width, height and depth of God's love, 19 and to know the Messiah's love that surpasses knowledge, so you may be filled with all the fullness of God.

We know that God loves us. Our beginning as believers has been firmly established by God's love. We are rooted in His love for us. We sing the children's song, "Jesus loves me this I know." The first verse you learn is John 3:16: "For God so loved the world..." Modern worship songs emphasize over and over God's love for us: "Oh, how He loves us..." "I could sing of His love forever" and many more. And yet it is a great task for us to really comprehend the vastness of His love.

To comprehend His love is to have a complete understanding, a firm grasp of how expansive, limitless, infinite is His love. Paul prays that not only would the church mentally know of God's love but that they would apprehend, or personally grasp, the depth of God's love. There is no greater truth to grasp than to know that God loves you. No matter what you've done, where you are, how far you've wandered away, how deep your anger is toward Him, He loves you. You can never be unloved by God.

You must allow God to love you, to shower you with His abundance, to wait on Him to be your provider, your provision. This requires an inner spiritual strength provided only by the Holy Spirit. To know God's love you must live in faith. This is true also for the church.

Sometimes we miss God's love because we don't give Him the opportunity to love us. We do this by limiting our exposure to experiences requiring faith in God. To know how you are hindered, consider any "I can't" statements or "we can't" statements.
"I can't worship singing these songs"
"I can't help in that area"
"We can't do that here"
"I can't talk in public"

When we deny God the opportunity to show Himself through us we miss the chance to know His love. To experience His love. To be embraced by it. To be overwhelmed by it. Know today that God loves you. And God loves your church.

Spend some time today contemplating God's love for you. Listen to some of the great songs that speak to His love for you. Take this opportunity to simply rest in the middle of His love. Don't think about implications of it, application to other things; just be still and content in the middle of His great love. Let His love wash over your soul today.

Pray:
Lord, thank You for loving me and for loving Your church. Thank You for sending Your Son. Thank You for blessing us. Thank You for being patient. Thank You for sending Your Spirit. I know You love me. I know You

love my church. Remind me all day today how much You love me and my church.

DAY 21
LORD, FILL YOUR CHURCH WITH YOUR LOVE

Ephesians 3:17-19

17 and that the Messiah may dwell in your hearts through faith. I pray that you, being rooted and firmly established in love, 18 may be able to comprehend with all the saints what is the length and width, height and depth of God's love, 19 and to know the Messiah's love that surpasses knowledge, so you may be filled with all the fullness of God.

It is significant that in verse 18 Paul says he is praying that we might be able to comprehend "with all the saints." While he could just be talking about every believer understanding, it seems to make more sense that he is talking about how the love of God can only truly be understood in the midst of community. That is to say, the work of loving others builds within us a fuller comprehension of God's love for us.

When you struggle through the work of real forgiveness instead of simply walking away from conflict you begin to understand God's forgiving love for you. When you dive into the depths of a messy life with someone struggling to find redemption you begin to understand the work of Christ on earth. When you selflessly allow someone else to have a moment of glory you were hoping to be your own you begin to sense what it meant for Christ to give His ministry over to the disciples. You will not grasp God's love unless you commit to a community of faith and decide to work through the struggles of relationship.

Therefore, we pray not only for ourselves, but for the body of Christ to know the expanse of God's love. This is a selfless prayer, not asking for ourselves alone but for the whole of the church. We need the church to grasp the love of Christ. The lost world needs the church to grasp the love of Christ. I need the rest of the church to know His love so that they might be patient with me. You need the church to grasp the love of Christ so that they will forgive you for your shortcomings in the body.

As we grasp that love by living it out with one another, the church becomes a beacon in a dark world. Remember Jesus' words in John 13:35, "By this all people will know that you are My disciples, if you have love for one another." When we love one another with the love of Christ we are accomplishing the mission.

This means we love through conflict and we love when it costs us personally. It means we love during crisis and we love when the person is unrepentant. Not until we are willing to love with the depth of His love will we experience all the fullness of God.

Pray today that God will pour His love out through your church. Pray that the practice of love will be more important than anything else. Pray that God will show you how to love others in the church. Warning: if you pray for God to love through you He will give you many opportunities to act with love instead of selfishness.

Pray:

Lord, today I pray for our church to be a place filled with Your love. Remind us to love through the conflict that always comes in relationships. Give us a deep love for one another that binds us together. Pour out Your love among us. Show me ways to love others this week. Help me to love those who hurt me, who are unrepentant, who are hard to love.

_____

_____

_____

_____

_____

DAY 22
LORD, TO YOU BE GLORY IN YOUR CHURCH

Ephesians 3:20-21

20 Now to Him who is able to do above and beyond all that we ask or think according to the power that works in us— 21 to Him be glory in the church and in Christ Jesus to all generations, forever and ever. Amen.

God chooses to use human vessels to accomplish His will. These human vessels are filled with His Spirit who works to do His will. For some strange reason He has chosen to use us, yielded to Him, to reach others in our situation. He does this not because He must or because it is most effective, but because He has chosen to. Even then, working through such weak vessels, God is able to do abundantly more than we can imagine. Don't limit yourself to seeing this as a materialistic dream or a "numbers" dream, but that God will use you and your church to accomplish more than you can imagine.

His dream for you is more than you can even consider. The church will do its best to have a good organization that functions well and involves as many as possible. But that isn't the goal. The goal is for the Lord to gain glory in the church. The only way that happens is if He does things beyond human thought or imagination or ability.

The beauty of this dream is that it is not limited to your ability or the resources of your church. The Lord works according to His power. As we saw in Ephesians 1, this is the same power that raised Christ from the dead and seated Him at the right hand of the Father. His work is done by His power. His vision for your church and your life is according to His power, not yours.

Because it is His vision and His power, He is the one who rightly gets the glory. It is His love that fills the church. It is His Spirit who indwells the church. It is His strength that sustains the church. To Him be the glory.

Let's covenant together to seek Him and to be filled by Him so that He might do what He wants through us all. And then, when He has worked, it will be obvious that He has done it because it will be more than we even imagined. At that point, there will be no one else deserving of glory. All credit, all glory will go to Him. We don't want to just do what people can do. We want God to do what only He can do. We want Him to receive the glory. To Him be glory in the church. To Him be glory in your life. To Him be glory in His church. Amen.

Pray:
Lord, to the One who is able to do above and beyond all that we ask or think, according to the power that works in us—to You be glory in the church and in Christ Jesus to all generations, forever and ever. Amen.

DAY 23
LORD, HELP YOUR CHURCH STAND

Ephesians 6:10-13

10 Finally, be strengthened by the Lord and by His vast strength. 11 Put on the full armor of God so that you can stand against the tactics of the Devil. 12 For our battle is not against flesh and blood, but against the rulers, against the authorities, against the world powers of this darkness, against the spiritual forces of evil in the heavens. 13 This is why you must take up the full armor of God, so that you may be able to resist in the evil day and having prepared everything, to take your stand.

The life of a believer and the activity of the church require the hand of God to be active. Dependence upon God is a non-negotiable. This is not just for salvation but for every day of life.

The verb in verse 10 is a passive tense, "be strengthened." We need the Lord to act on our lives to make us strong. He does this from the reserve of His infinite strength. We do not extract strength from a small pool but from the vast ocean of God's resource. Pray for your church to be strengthened by the Lord because His strength is required.

It is required because every church is involved in spiritual warfare. The Devil is always on the attack against the church. Although defeated, he is not going away quietly. He is always lurking, looking for ways to deceive, distract and destroy the church. He will use every tactic at his disposal to tear down the testimony of the church. He will work every day to get the church involved in things that are good but not gospel. He influences humans to question one another's motives and sincerity. He relishes turning us against one another, seeing each other as the enemy instead of him. He is a roaring lion seeking to devour (1 Peter 5:8).

Paul states clearly that there is an ongoing battle with the forces of evil, with powers in high places, with authorities that are much greater, more devious than we can imagine. To enter into this battle we must be strengthened by the Lord and protected with His armor. We will talk about the armor in the next couple of days. Today we begin with the end of the battle, just as Paul does.

Paul exhorts and encourages the church to stand in the strength and armor of God. In verse 11 he exhorts us to put on the armor and in verse 13 he brings encouragement by saying: Once you have put on the armor you will be able to resist and you will stand. Our prayer today is that the church will stand against the attacks of the enemy. We know the universal Church will not be deterred (Matthew 16:18), but we also know that local churches have at times succumbed to defeat at the hands of the enemy.

There is a battle ongoing today. Pray for your church to be strengthened, to be armored and to stand. Pray that the Lord would protect your church, that He would defeat the plans of Satan. Pray that your church would prepare for the battle and would stand strong with the Lord.

Pray:
Lord, strengthen our church with Your strength. Pour out your strength in us when we are weak and tempted.

Lord protect our church with Your armor. Help us to stand against the trials that come against us. Make us strong, reliant upon You. Lord defeat our enemies and help us to rightly identify our enemies. Reveal the traps Satan has set and keep us from falling.

_____

_____

_____

_____

_____

DAY 24
LORD, PREPARE YOUR CHURCH

Ephesians 6:13-17

13 This is why you must take up the full armor of God, so that you may be able to resist in the evil day and having prepared everything, to take your stand. 14 Stand, therefore,
with truth like a belt around your waist,
righteousness like armor on your chest,
15 and your feet sandaled with readiness for the gospel of peace.
16 In every situation take the shield of faith, and with it you will be able to extinguish all the flaming arrows of the evil one.
17 Take the helmet of salvation,
and the sword of the Spirit, which is God's word.

Over the next two days we are going to pray through the armor of God on behalf of the church. It's important to remember that we need the full, or whole, armor of God. It is not sufficient to put on some of the armor, we need every piece to protect ourselves and others. We need this armor because the church is in the midst of a massive spiritual battle that has endured for millennia. Do not think that somehow your church will be exempt or spared. Do not think that by ignoring it you will not be affected. The battle is ongoing today. It is time to engage the enemy by putting on the armor.

The first piece of the armor is the belt of truth. Truth serves as the foundation for the armor just as it is the foundation for the Christian life. The enemy will attack with lies, half-truths and distortions. He will convince people of lies about one another that seem outlandish, yet some will fall prey to this deception. He will lead the church to accept half-truths that are more convenient that the full truth. He will distort the truth to satisfy selfish desires or to rationalize sinful acts.

Pray for your church to be firmly committed to the truth of God's word and the truth of God's justice. Keeping the belt of truth fastened signifies a commitment to trusting in God's word and living by God's word. It also shows a desire to seek justice when the truth is difficult or causes embarrassment. It is always right to do the right thing, even when it is painful. Pray that your church is committed to doing the right thing, to living in truth and by truth.

The belt of truth is closely related to the breastplate of righteousness. As a believer your righteousness comes from Christ and this is what assures you of salvation. You cannot be righteous on your own. You are dependent upon His righteousness to gain entry into His presence. This positional righteousness in Christ, that you are found in Christ at all times, does not mean that you have no need of living a life based on practical righteousness. If your daily life abandons any desire to seek right living then you give Satan multiple openings of attack on you and the church.

Pray that God would protect the walk of every believer in your church. Pray they would seek to walk with Christ, living in righteousness. Righteous living means living out the salvation God has poured into us. Pray that the pastor, staff and lay leaders would live in obedience to God's call on their life. We have seen in the past how influential the public failings of church leaders have been on the effectiveness of the church. Pray that every leader in the church would walk with God.

Then pray for the gospel witness of the church. Pray that the church would be fully committed to sharing the gospel with the world on a daily basis. Pray that God would open doors of evangelistic opportunities for your church today. Pray that the church would be ready to speak the gospel of peace to a world mired in chaos and despair. Pray that your church would be a light shining in darkness.

Pray:
Lord, we are in a battle and we need your armor to stand firm. Lord, keep us from lies and deceit. Lord, help us stand with Your truth all around us. Lord protect our hearts from sin. Guard our lives from missing Your will. Protect our leaders from moral failure. Lord open doors for us to take the gospel this week. Lord, make us bold witnesses for Your sake.

_____

_____

_____

_____

_____

DAY 25
LORD, PREPARE YOUR CHURCH

Ephesians 6:13-17

13 This is why you must take up the full armor of God, so that you may be able to resist in the evil day and having prepared everything, to take your stand. 14 Stand, therefore,
with truth like a belt around your waist,
righteousness like armor on your chest,
15 and your feet sandaled with readiness for the gospel of peace.
16 In every situation take the shield of faith, and with it you will be able to extinguish all the flaming arrows of the evil one.
17 Take the helmet of salvation,
and the sword of the Spirit, which is God's word.

The ruler of this world will launch fiery darts of doubt, temptation, lust, despair, anger, frustration, bitterness, heartache, struggle and trials into our lives. For many people these darts strike at the heart and leave them helpless against the enemy. They succumb to each one with more eagerness each day until they are mired deep in their own pool of sin.

The only protection from these darts is the shield of faith, trusting in the Lord, His word and His work. Faith is a total dependence upon God and a willingness to do His will. Merely showing up to a service and going through the motions of religion is not sufficient faith to defend against the attacks of the enemy. Saying nice words and wearing clean clothes will not protect you from Satan's darts. We must be a people of living faith.

Living faith directs our lives as believers and is that upon which we lean in the face of temptation or rebellion. Pray for your church to be infused with living faith. Pray for your church to trust the person of Christ and not just to go through the motions of church. Pray that your church will be dependent upon Him and committed to following His will. Pray that they lean on Christ when the attacks from Satan come. Pray that they respond to temptation with faith and not doubt. Pray that they love following more than rebelling.

A helmet protects your head which means it protects your very life. Those who wear the helmet of salvation have no fear of death because they are assured of their eternal fate. With your life securely in the hands of the Father you can live in this life with confidence, knowing that nothing can affect your eternity. Pray that your church not fear anything in this world. Political elections, government intervention, poverty, hardship and becoming a social leper cannot keep us from following the Lord because we know how our story will end. Pray that your church puts its hope in Christ and not in society or government. Pray that your church always seeks His kingdom and follows His will even when it makes life more difficult.

Finally, pray for your church to elevate God's word above all else. The only weapon in the armor is the sword of the Spirit, God's word. Pray that God's word remains important to your church. Pray for those who teach the word. Pray for your small group Bible study leaders. Pray that they would remain true to the word. Pray that the word would permeate every corner of the church and every activity. Pray that His word would be the standard for how the church operates, how it responds to crisis, how it reaches the community and how it worships.

Pray:
Lord, we need Your strength and Your armor to withstand the attacks of the enemy. Deepen our trust in You every day. Show us how to trust You and how to follow You. Make us bold in our obedience to You. Keep us confident in Your promises. Lord, may Your word intrude into every area of our church life. We want to know You and we want to keep Your word faithfully.

_____

_____

_____

_____

_____

DAY 26
LORD, HELP YOUR CHURCH

Ephesians 6:18

18 Pray at all times in the Spirit with every prayer and request and stay alert in this with all perseverance and intercession for all the saints.

If we were completely honest we would all admit that the large amount of emphasis in our prayer time is spent on personal requests. While we probably spend too much time proportionally on this, presenting requests to God is an important part of praying for your church.

Paul encouraged the church to spend time praying for one another, for special needs in the body of Christ. We feel a deep, intense need, therefore, we go before God and petition, that is, pour out our soul to God. Need—great need—confronts us and the only possible help and deliverance is God. Therefore, we come and lay our need before Him as a child: crying, pleading and begging for His help, comfort, deliverance and peace.

Notice the four "all's" in this verse. Pray all the time. Pray in the Spirit for every (all) things. Pray with all perseverance. Pray for all the saints. Prayer is the all-consuming work of the believer.

"All Times" – Just as Paul tells the Thessalonian church to "pray constantly" (I Thessalonians 5:17), he tells the Ephesians to "pray at all times." We must be ready at all times to communicate with the Lord. We need to keep the lines of communication open and take things to Him in the moment, not waiting for the evening or next morning. This spiritual activity should be like breathing. We are constantly aware of His presence and His sovereignty over every minute.

"Every Prayer" – God is interested in every prayer, every request. He cares about every aspect of our lives. He wants to be involved in the deepest corners of our existence. Present every request to Him.

"All Perseverance and Intercession" – Prayer is an intense spiritual activity. Praying for others, presenting requests to the Lord, requires much from us. Have you ever gotten distracted while praying? Have you ever fallen asleep while in prayer? Then you know how difficult it is to spend time praying. To pray for others requires perseverance. Keep on asking. Keep on seeking. When you get off track, get back on track. When you wake up, go back to praying.

"All the Saints" – Prayer is needed for all believers everywhere. There is never an end to the spiritual battles others are going through and we should pray for them. Physical, emotional, social and spiritual needs are real and we should not fail to present these needs to the Lord.

As you go forward I suggest you begin using some type of prayer journal. It can be as simple as a spiral notebook but you need something to begin listing your requests and God's answers. You might create sections for family, personal, church, friends, work, school, etc. Find a way that works for you to list needs, both ongoing and temporal. Put a date by requests and go back through to see how God has answered. If you are just beginning, don't be too ambitious with this project. Start simple and let it grow as you grow.

As you pray today start your list, if you haven't already. Begin praying simply for those needs you are aware of and continue by being more aware when others ask for prayer.

Pray:
Lord, You know the needs within our church, my family and my own life. I place all these requests before You today. You are the answer to all of them. I pray that You would be glorified in each situation. Do Your work to accomplish Your will.

_____

_____

_____

_____

_____

DAY 27
LORD, MAKE YOUR CHURCH BOLD

Ephesians 6:19-20

19 Pray also for me, that the message may be given to me when I open my mouth to make known with boldness the mystery of the gospel. 20 For this I am an ambassador in chains. Pray that I might be bold enough in Him to speak as I should.

In one of the most amazing passages in Ephesians, the apostle Paul, the greatest teacher, church planter and evangelist in the history of the church, asks the simple believers of Ephesus to pray for him to be a bold witness. Paul, the teacher, asks his students to pray for him. Paul, the church planter, NEEDS his church plant to pray for him. Paul, the evangelist, requests help to open his mouth and be bold with the gospel. If Paul needs this prayer, how much more does your church, your pastor, your Bible study leader, your membership need prayer for boldness?

Paul's desire was to share the gospel in the same manner as Jesus. In Mark 8:32 it says: "He was openly talking about this." Jesus was openly talking about his own suffering to come, the crucifixion and resurrection. The word translated "openly" is the same word used by Paul in Ephesians 6:19-20 that is translated "boldness" and "bold." Paul wanted to speak openly about the gospel. He wanted to speak like Jesus spoke.

This prayer for the church is not that it would be obnoxious and loud, but that the church would speak openly about the gospel. Too often the church acts muzzled, as if we cannot speak. The truth for most believers in the West is that we can speak but we do not speak. We are self-muzzled. We have quieted ourselves.

Pray for your church to be bold, to speak openly about the gospel. This means including the gospel in regular conversations. Make the truth of Christ as much a part of your conversation at work as it is at church. Paul requested this prayer; there is no shame in admitting that you also need this prayer.

Paul makes this request while he is in chains for preaching the gospel, yet he is not willing to be quiet about his faith. He is surely tempted to lay low for a while, maybe let the anger of the authorities subside. But he still wants to make the gospel known "as I should." Even against great odds, Paul prays for boldness to share. In the face of ongoing persecution, he prays to speak openly the mystery of the gospel.

Pray for your church to be bold in sharing the gospel. Pray that your church would openly proclaim the truth of Jesus, the redemption found only in Him, as it should. Pray that your church would gladly live and love the gospel message of forgiveness and that it would walk through whatever persecution follows for the opportunity to talk about Jesus. Pray again for your pastor and your teachers. Pray for those who will have opportunities this week to share the gospel. Pray that they will open their mouths and speak. Pray for missionaries sent and supported by your church, that they would be bold in Him to share the love of Christ on the cross.

Pray:

Lord, make Your church bold to share the gospel this week. Give us words to speak and courage to open our mouths to share your gospel with others. Help us speak openly about the love found in Christ alone and about Your great work on our behalf. Lord, we will not be ashamed of the gospel for it is the power of God unto salvation.

DAY 28
LORD, GIVE YOUR CHURCH DISCERNMENT

Philippians 1:9-11

9 And I pray this: that your love will keep on growing in knowledge and every kind of discernment, 10 so that you can approve the things that are superior and can be pure and blameless in the day of Christ, 11 filled with the fruit of righteousness that comes through Jesus Christ to the glory and praise of God.

The church in Philippi is one of Paul's favorite of all those he planted. From humble beginnings the church became a model of generosity, faith, joy and sacrifice. In this first chapter of Philippians Paul's prayer is for maturity for the entire body of Christ. All the pronouns used here are plural. He is praying for the body of Christ to be mature, not just for individual members.

Maturity begins with love that grows in knowledge as we've previously discussed. Here Paul adds discernment to knowledge and he pairs it with love. This may seem like an odd combination, to pray that love will grow in discernment, but Paul knows that Christian love is not blind love any more than Christian faith is blind faith. The heart and mind work together.

Paul wants the church to be able to aptly distinguish the things that are superior from those that are inferior. The church must distinguish that which is valuable, pure, holy from that which is vacuous, immoral and vain. Notwithstanding what the culture may say, making these judgments is loving. The church should call others to live more nobly, selflessly and decently. We must make judgments on what is noble, what is selfless, what is decent. This discernment must come from the One who determines truth, not from our own flawed value system.

To stand aside while parents devalue their children or while communities exalt the shameful is not loving toward the community. The church is in a unique position to lead the culture toward those things that are magnificent, dignified and gracious. It is the church that has insight into that which honors God and exalts His righteous good.

Pray for your church to be discerning in their love. Pray that they will grow in their ability to discern what is superior and will courageously exalt those things that are pure and blameless. Pray that your church will steadily walk into maturity.

Because these are plural nouns our prayer is for the body of Christ. For the body to mature, obviously individual members must be growing in their love, knowledge and discernment. But those members must also be growing together in their love, knowledge and discernment. Church maturity means that the members are growing alongside one another, involved in community and committed to the maturity of the body as a whole. Pray for your church to grow together, as one. Pray for them to mature as a body. Pray for the community to be valued among the members.

Pray:
Lord, grow the love of our church for one another and for You. Help our church grow up together in maturity so that we might discern those things that are superior. Teach us how to exalt the noble and good. Show us Your

righteousness and lead us to stand courageously for that which is right and honorable. Lord, we pray for the community of our church. Grow us together. Help us love one another. Convict us of the sins that lead to division: gossip, bitterness, jealousy, envy and holding grudges.

_____

_____

_____

_____

_____

DAY 29
LORD, GIVE YOUR CHURCH JOY

Philippians 4:4-7

4 Rejoice in the Lord always. I will say it again: Rejoice! 5 Let your graciousness be known to everyone. The Lord is near. 6 Don't worry about anything, but in everything, through prayer and petition with thanksgiving, let your requests be made known to God. 7 And the peace of God, which surpasses every thought, will guard your hearts and minds in Christ Jesus.

Paul closes his letter to the church in Philippi with several emphatic exhortations. Rejoice! Be gracious to all. Don't worry. Pray!

The church ought to be a place of rejoicing. Not every day is a happy day, but even then the believer has reason to rejoice. Paul writes from prison and says: Rejoice in the Lord ALWAYS! These weren't just words for Paul and the Philippians knew it. When Paul was in prison in Philippi he prayed and sang (Acts 16). There is always a reason to rejoice because no matter what we are going through the Lord is with us. He will carry us. He will never leave or forsake us.

We live in a world filled with false hope where people search daily for some reason to be happy. Disappointed at every turn, they escape into alcohol, drugs, promiscuous sex, non-stop entertainment on their smart phone and shallow friendships on facebook. The church should provide a powerful answer in this search for happiness. The church should be filled with those determined to rejoice in all circumstances. We should encourage one another toward joy. The alternative to joy is bitterness and selfishness. The child of God should not go through life with a sour look.

I like the way J. Vernon McGee says it in his commentary on Philippians: "I have thought it would be nice if churches could have an attitude adjustment hour. Here comes Mrs. Brown. She has just heard some choice gossip during the week and she can hardly wait to spread it around in the church. Wouldn't it be wonderful to take her into an attractive room and have a cup of coffee with her and get her into a sweet mood of rejoicing in the Lord so she would not go around spreading her gossip? Here comes Deacon Jones, breathing fire like a dragon because something doesn't suit him. It would be nice to take him to that room and help him recover his cool so he could go in and enjoy the sermon. We need an attitude adjustment hour, a happy hour, in the church. Frankly, the Devil has gotten in his licks -- he has made folk believe they can't have fun going to church and I think they can. I think it ought to be a joyful place and a place of power" (Thru The Bible with J. Vernon McGee, by J. Vernon McGee).

Pray for your church to be a place filled with rejoicing. This is not a call to pretend the world is easy, or to push aside the struggles, but to not allow our outward circumstance to determine our inward attitude. The Lord does not change. He always keeps His promises. His character can always be trusted. His presence is always with us. His love is never ending. His patience is enduring. Rejoice in the Lord.

One of the ways to rejoice in all circumstances is to look outward to help others. Be gracious to others. Be generous to them. Your church should always err on the side of generosity and graciousness. The opposite would be stinginess and legalism. These are hard ways to live. Pray for your church to be a giving church, a generous church. Pray for your church to be filled with graciousness to those who are failing, to those who are struggling. Pray for your church to be joyful.

Pray:
Lord, fill our church with Your joy. Remind us daily of Your promises, Your provision and Your presence. Make us generous to others and gracious to all. Lord, show us how You have met our needs and teach us to rejoice in the midst of our difficulties.

DAY 30
LORD, GIVE YOUR CHURCH PEACE

Philippians 4:4-7

4 Rejoice in the Lord always. I will say it again: Rejoice! 5 Let your graciousness be known to everyone. The Lord is near. 6 Don't worry about anything, but in everything, through prayer and petition with thanksgiving, let your requests be made known to God. 7 And the peace of God, which surpasses every thought, will guard your hearts and minds in Christ Jesus.

"Don't worry about anything."

Paul is not saying that we have nothing to worry about. He isn't saying that the believer has no problems, never gets sick, will always have a job and will be exempt from hardship. Paul isn't saying that the church will not suffer persecution, will have plenty of financial resources and will always be unified. He is exhorting the church to present all of these potential worries to God.

Praying is the antidote to worry. Praying affords the believer with the opportunity to say, "I'm not worried because I've already talked to God about it." That does not mean that God will work everything out to our satisfaction or pleasure. It also does not obligate God to resolve things in a timely manner suitable to our personal schedule. It does mean that we will trust the

Lord and know that He cares, He loves and He is able to deal with these things better than we are.

So pour out your heart to the Lord. Share with Him your struggles, your pain, your doubts and your temptations so that He may give you victory, healing, assurance and strength. Let Him know of your worries and allow Him to bring you peace. Confess to Him your sins so that He might forgive and restore you.

Opening the depth of your heart to the Lord, the intimate details that you think are hidden, will allow you to experience His love for you at a new intensity. He loves you. He desires to support and restore you, not to condemn you. As you put your problems at His feet, let them go and do not pick them back up. Leave them with Him. He will deal with them in the providence of His will. This is His promise to you.

Pray for your church to be a praying church. Beyond the opening and closing prayers at meetings, pray that your church is filled with prayer warriors. Your church needs believers calling out to the Lord on behalf of one another.

Because of His promises, we can present our requests with thanksgiving. This is not a throwaway term in the middle of verse 6. He is trustworthy. You can thank Him today for answers that won't come until next week or next year.

Therefore, once we present our requests, we have peace. No matter how large the problem, no matter how challenging the crisis, He is able. Trust Him and be at peace.

There is more than one kind of peace mentioned in the Bible. When you give your life to Christ you are forgiven and you are at peace with God. When we are all getting along with one another there is peace in the body of Christ. One day there will be world peace when the Lord returns. In verse 7 he speaks of the peace that passes understanding. This is a peace that comes by faith when we pray through everything that worries us. In the midst of turmoil, upheaval, chaos and frustration, God gives us peace. Present your requests to the Lord, trust Him and be at peace.

Pray for your church to have this peace that passes understanding. This means you pray for your church to trust the Lord. Pray for your church to actively go to the Lord first instead of last. Pray for your church to seek His will and be content with His answers.

Pray:
Lord, I give You my worries. I trust You with my hurts. Take my doubts and my failures. I know you hold my future. Lord, help my church seek Your peace. Help us trust You in everything. Grow our faith as we go through stressful times and fill us with Your peace.

_____

_____

_____

_____

_____

CONTINUING TO PRAY FOR YOUR CHURCH

Pray for your pastor and staff and families by name:

_____

_____

_____

_____

_____

Pray for small group leaders by name:

_____

_____

_____

_____

_____

Pray for your church:

Bring the Lord Glory	John 17:1-5
Have the Lord's Vision	John 17:1-5
Be Protected	John 17:6-15
Be Sanctified	John 17:14-19
Be United	John 17:20-26
Be Filled with Knowledge of God	Colossians 1:9
Grow – Bearing Fruit	Colossians 1:10
Be Strengthened	Colossians 1:11-12
Be Burdened for the Lost	Colossians 1:13-14
Give Thanks for Your Church	Ephesians 1:15-16
The Lord Reveal Himself	Ephesians 1:17
Open the Eyes of the Church	Ephesians 1:18-19
Find Our Hope in the Lord	Ephesians 1:18-19
Know Our Place with the Lord	Ephesians 1:18-19
Unleash His Power	Ephesians 1:20-21
Bless Our Pastor	Ephesians 3:14-16
Dwell in Our Church	Ephesians 3:17
Fill Our Church with Love	Ephesians 3:17-19
To You be Glory in Our Church	Ephesians 3:20-21
Help Our Church Stand	Ephesians 6:10-13
Lord, Arm Our Church	Ephesians 6:13-17
Help Our Church	Ephesians 6:18
Make Our Church Bold	Ephesians 6:19-20
Give Our Church Discernment	Philippians 1:9-11
Give Our Church Joy	Philippians 4:4-5
Give Our Church Peace	Philippians 4:6-7

Special Requests for your church (Think of events, issues, visions for the future, individuals, ongoing ministries):